DEDICATION

For my mama and grandmamas. My sister, my cousins, and my aunties, too..

"When I think of unconditional love, I think of God's love, followed by the love of a loving mother. The type of love that is lifelong, timeless, and can't be given by any other. A type of love that is patient, understanding, and loves through and through. The type of love that will always remain, despite the circumstances of you..."

The Closest Thing to God's Love, Cherish

For my sweet baby girl..

"Into my seed I vow to sew love, joy, peace, patience, and all things pure and true. I promise to invest my best, and I pray that all that is good in me be great in you. For my sweet child, I will be gentle, faithful, and practice self-control. My responsibility to you inspires me to be better in all ways, and with you, I will continue to grow..."

Family Tree, Cherish

I wrote Rooted while learning how to sit with myself—with memory, with faith, with grief, and with the quiet work of healing. Some of these poems were born from heartbreak, others from prayer, and many from the space in between where I didn't yet have answers, only honesty.

If you see yourself in these pages, know this: healing is not linear, growth is not loud, and becoming takes time. May these words meet you where you are and remind you that restoration is possible— slowly, tenderly, and on purpose.

Table of Contents

Journal Entries excluded from TOC.

ROOTED

"Then Christ will make His home in your hearts as you trust in Him. Your roots will grow down into God's love and keep you strong."

Ephesians 3:17, NLT

Rooted

I am rooted.

Just as a tree.

I am rooted in love, I am rooted in my beliefs.

And that is how come,

or should I say,

That is why

I have the wisdom not to stray.

At least not too far away.

From the roots.

The roots in which were grounded for me.

Long before me.

Where I'm From

I am from pictures.
From TCB relaxers,
leaving big, icky scabs on my scalp,
waiting to be peeled.
I am from the mud cakes
and mud pies sitting in my backyard.
I am from the breeze rattling the leaves on the trees as I
sit and chat with my cousins on the front porch.
I am from family cook-outs and strong, fierce attitudes
stemming from Joe and Pearl.
I am from the grooves and goofiness that flow through
my family's veins.
I am from "don't talk back" and "stop runnin' in and out
that door!"
I am from Sunday dinner: fried chicken, white rice, and
collard greens.
But most of all, I am from the beautiful Grimes and
Cleveland genes!

-Young Nae, 2002

Geneazodiology (4 Pisces)

I am a Pisces,
Who was made by a Pisces that got with a Pisces,
Created a Pisces,
Then later wed a Pisces.
That is he.

I am a Pisces,
Who was made by a Pisces that got with a Pisces,
Created a Pisces,
Then later wed a Sagittarius.
That is she.

I am a Pisces created by Pisces
Who was head-over-heels for a Sagittarius,
Then later got with a Pisces,
And created a Sagittarius.
That is we.

I am a Pisces.
That is me.

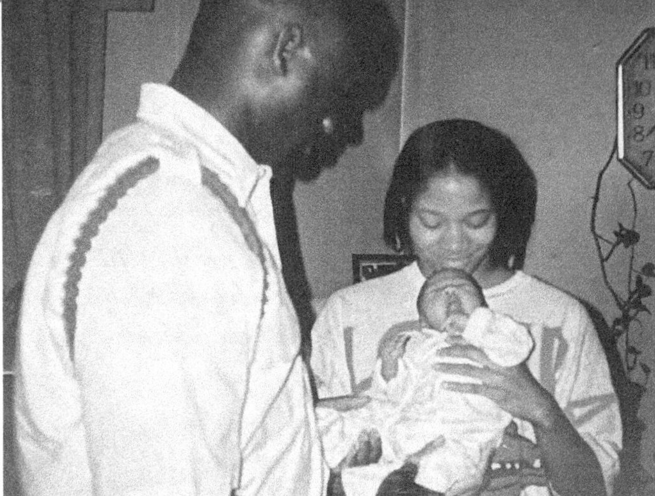

Dad, Mam, and me

Mama, Granny, and I

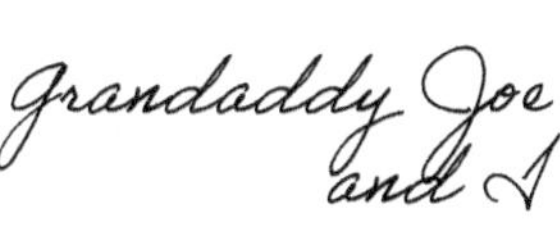

Grandaddy Joe and I

JOURNAL ENTRY

"...Grandaddy Joe put on my tire today. I'm glad he found one sooner than later. He got it for cheap, too, lol.. I love him so much. He is always there when I need him."

"Ova Dey"

\- SaVernacular (Savannah "Sea Pote" Vernacular)

Dey: they, there, their.

Ex 1: "Da churn said dey don't wanna go ova dey to dey grandma house 'cause it's too hot to be sittin' on a plastic sofa."
Ex 2: "I'm from ova dey, down by dat wata."

BROKEN

"You are what you speak.. What are you saying when you are not around people?"

JOURNAL ENTRY

"It's really been five, going on six years since I've taken time to write in this journal. I'm so glad that I still have it. Reading over some of my older entries, I'm not sure whether I was in a better space then or now. To be honest with myself, I haven't grown much, and I haven't accomplished much in six years. My life is passing me by. I don't have much motivation, and some days I feel like I'm just here, lost, confused, and misguided. I'm getting too old to keep making the same mistakes, so hopefully I can find some inspiration getting back into my writing. Some things have changed since I last wrote. I quit my job and went back to my old one.

Definitely not one of my greatest decisions, but I have to live with it now. I don't 100% regret it, but at times I wish I'd stayed in place. I was being money-hungry. I miss the feeling of prestige associated with being an employee of a Fortune 50 company. But anyway, things are what they are now, so no point in focusing on what could have been. So, here I am, a 26-year-old store manager, currently laid off due to COVID-19, still with the same unaccomplished goals, and still involved in a relationship with an uncertain future. My life sucks, and I've been broken. I blame others for my unhappiness when I have many issues I need to deal with within myself. My Grandaddy Joe left us on 8/31/2017, and it has forever changed my life. So in an effort not to feel like sh*t every day, I will write."

This piece was written circa 2010/2011, as I lay on the floor in my cousin's bedroom. I wrote this poem because, at the time, I was going through the motions of an old relationship, not knowing that the same motions would prevail even more in my next relationship(s) to come. A cycle...

A Victim of Circumstance

Spoken over Rama Duke's 'We Rise'

A victim of circumstance.

Giving love a 1st, 2nd, and a 333rd chance.

You wouldn't forget if you could,

But Lord knows that you should.

And all the things that you do,

only result from the sh*t that you've been through.

You've been fed so many lies

that you don't recognize the taste of the truth.

You were wishing for love, but only stringed along for lustful use.

Now you trying to refuse all the years of mental abuse,

Girl if you

Give your all to one that'll be everything they take from you.

Now your heart is broken and you can't seem to put it back together.

Alone you stand, you're thinking you'll never find nothing better

You were smart enough to leave; you think staying made you stronger.

The nights of hell carried on, and somehow

you wanted them to last longer.

You're saying "times will get better"

and you're wishing that he would change,

But girl, your lover is a fiend and he's addicted to the game

So now you're trying to comprehend,

and you're constantly asking him "Why?"

As he's holding in his laughter, he amuses at your cries.

You had a smile so warm, turned to a smile so cold

And you have a soul so young, but you living life like you're so old.

Now your new boo, he just can't seem to understand.

He's like baby, "How can you do these things that you possibly can?"

Expressing your feelings seems impossible, but you feel that it's true

However, the doubt wanders in your mind

when he replies to "love you too."

See, the past dwells in the present whenever we try not to let it,

And the more you try to, the more we can't seem to forget it.

 It's like an old addiction, but it's a brand-new drug,

You told yourself never again & ended up back at love… D*mn

You're just a victim of circumstance.

And even though you're afraid of love, his love, new love, it's something you seem to need and

It eases your mind like a dime bag of that good weed, and

Somehow, you're hoping you won't be hurt again,

but ironically, it's what you expect.

So, you just try to make the best memories of the times you share now,

with hopes that you won't regret...

'Cause you know you won't forget.

Inconsistent Love

Just can't get enough of–
That inconsistent love.
Because it's not enough, love.

JOURNAL ENTRY

"I wasn't really planning on writing, but decided to jot down a lil something. I have a lot running through my mind, so I really don't know what to say/write. I honestly just need a fresh start. I pray that I get a clear mind, Lord knows I need it. I feel so confused sometimes..."

At this time in my life, I was going through heartbreak again. I was chasing love so bad, I went all the way from Savannah to New York, thinking I had found it. In hindsight, I realize that I was breaking my own heart more than any man had.

Banking on Heartbreak

Dear God,

I really don't know what to say,

so I ask that you hear my heart.

I'm trying to find the words to speak,

but my lips can't seem to part.

These emotions come so quick and mixed,

I don't even know where to start.

The advice that was given to me years ago,

I wish I could go back and take.

And maybe, just maybe,

I'd be free from the heartbreak.

I have been hurt. I have been betrayed.

I've been used, disappointed and broken.

A lot of damage from spoken words.

A lot of resentment from words unspoken.

If healing were a piggy bank,

I'd give it my last token.

What kind of deal is it to get everything you want but lose yourself in the process?

Broken

I have been broken,
and I need some real healing.
I am heavy and stretched thin.
Heavy with burden. Heavy with worry.
Heavy with sin.
Heavy from carrying my past.
My past mistakes and failures.
Somehow, I still manage to give my time,
energy, and my not-quite-best.
Confused with the illusion of being blessed.
I'm stressed.
I'm blessed?
God don't bless no mess.
Single-momma.
Navigating through trauma.
The trauma of my mama, her mama,
and her mama's mama's mama.
Generational curses will still, somehow, end with me.
I pray angelic protection over my seed.
On the road to recovery.

Lost

I've been lost for a while now
Broken. Confused.
Everyday I feel I get further
Further
And further away
From where I am supposed to be.
I can't help but to be so disappointed in me.
I get the word every Sunday
Yet, I am still at a distance from God.
Temptation is easy, discipline is hard.
Lord, fix my soul and heal my heart.
I'm so tired of living like this.
Every day I wake up, feeling so purposeless.

FAITHFULLY FRACTURED

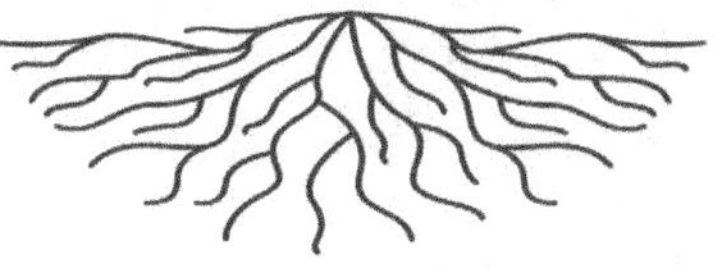

Waiting, Craving

I crave the unique intimacy
that only an equally yoked pair could share.
The love shared
between a woman and her man.
Praying to God,
I'm doing my best to be as patient as I can.
But it gets lonely at times.
I know I'm not alone, but I feel alone sometimes..
My future, my love,
I've been praying for you.
I've waited this long, guess I'll keep waiting for you.
Lord, give me the courage
To not be discouraged.

I am HER

I speak with confidence.
I walk with a stride.
I handle my business.
I enjoy the ride.
I will defeat any feat
that presents itself against me.
I love, I act,
I think intentionally.
Today is a new day,
a new start,
a new light.

What's done is done;
I do what's right.

Perfect, I am not,
but faithful, I am.

JOURNAL ENTRY

"..I woke up about 2 AM this morning and had a poem in my head. 'Inconsistent Love'... whoo! That's a shout all in itself, lol. I was too lazy to get out of bed and write, so when I get the time, I will write and come up with something. Now that I've talked with God this morning, I'm feeling really good. It's something about prayer that makes me feel relieved."

JOURNAL ENTRY

"I haven't written in here in a couple of weeks, and it's crazy because it seems like since I've stopped, my mind has been all over the place. What have I been up to? What have I been thinking? I've been inconsistent with my diet, working out, praying, and talking to God daily. Ron and I messed around. I know I said I wouldn't look back, but I just can't seem to stay away. Anyway, I'm considering attending school for literature or writing.

Whatever I decide, I'm just eager to start. I know I will be great, I won't have it any other way <3."

"I don't know anything at all.
And who am I to say you love me?
I don't know anything at all.
And who am I to say you need me?"

"Sometimes your biggest downfall can be another n***a's problems."
-Starlito *"Imposter Syndrome"*

JOURNAL ENTRY

As I began to fall back in love with myself, I realized that some of the things I spent a lot of my time doing didn't align with my spirit, my personal goals, or my inner self as a whole.

This bar stood out to me. When I first heard it, I immediately thought of identifying the "other person" so that I could place the blame for certain problems I've faced. But now, I am seeing that my old self was the other person. And the problems of this "other person" were, in fact, my own. The energy I once carried wasn't the energy intended for my true nature, and my biggest downfall was wasting too much time in spaces where I wasn't called to be. I was my own worst enemy.

"What you do now determines what you do later."

"There are years that ask questions, and years that answer."
-Zora Neale Hurston

BLOOM

"When you align, you will be divine."

JOURNAL ENTRY

"...So, yesterday I decided to block you-know-who from contacting me in any way. I figured it was pointless to follow him on Twitter because I'm always in my feelings behind his tweets. I still have hopes or a feeling that he'll come around, but I know that's not going to happen. Hopefully the feeling will fade away...I don't know where ima go when the lease is up. I'm trying to go everywhere BUT 808...I can't wait to have a man who loves me, makes me happy, and makes me whole. I know he's probably wishing the same thing for me right now, I'm waiting for you, boo <3.."

"The only lady I could ever match bonds with
On some atomic bond shit, our love is plutonic.
But I just can't put my foot on it.
My one and my only, we not only lovers but homies"

JOURNAL ENTRY

"I feel really good today, and I'm thankful that God has placed me in the position that I'm in. Sunday, I found a couple of old poems I wrote, which is awesome! I was hoping I would come across a few of them. I'll record them in here soon."

JOURNAL ENTRY

"Good morning! I've been up since about six this morning. I laid in the bed and talked to God, then I got up at seven and went for a light jog. I feel so good. I wonder if I'm doing this right? Is this what my book is supposed to be about? Idk. I'll continue to pray about it. I do enjoy writing. It relieves my mind a little bit."

JOURNAL ENTRY

"I'm currently watching Waiting to Exhale for the hundredth time in about three weeks.

I'm unsure why I've been so obsessed with this movie. I suppose it's because I can relate to some of the emotional struggles the women face. Sometimes, I wonder if I'm wrong to entertain other guys when he still has my heart. (sad, but true.) He acts like he's not bothered at all by our distance, but he'll feel it one day. I wonder what God thinks about me? Maybe I should ask?"

JOURNAL ENTRY

"Yesterday, I went for a walk and then came home to finish laundry. Sometimes, when I'm walking and see a person twice in one lap, I wonder how they can go so fast, and wish I was on their level! But, then it hits me, that I am on my own path, which makes me think about the same thing for my life. I am on my own path! And besides, if I'm seeing them twice, that means they are seeing me twice too."

Bad Hair Day

Why don't I like the fro look?

People be saying,
"Girl, I love when your hair is like that."

rolls eyes
As if it's my "glow" look.
folds arms

If it ain't straight
or if it ain't long,
I say issa "NO" look!
But I go and check the mirror again,
crack a lil' smile,
and I ROCK the fro look!

If I were the bag, my insecurities would be securin' me.

Insecure

I wish I had longer hair.

And I wish I had a rounder, a**
I got too much gut
And not enough cash
#thesearemyproblems

Dandelion

Cherish her. Cherish. The Cherisher.
Chile.
I am so fragile.
I have become aware of my emotions (?)
and the reasons why..
At this point,
I just need to apply.
I need to become in tune
and in control,
be in control,
come in control.
I am in control.
Handling me
with care, compassion, and consideration.
Safe travels.

This piece was written out of a moment of self-love. A reminder of the inner beauty I behold. A reminder to see me, the way God sees me.

Mirror

Why do you smile when you look at me?
I smile at your never-ending glow.
When our eyes meet, I see into your beautiful soul.
I see the multitude of sacrifices that you have made for me.
I smile at what the eyes cannot see.
Despite your flaws, I love you deeply, and far beyond those.
In a garden of tulips,
I smile upon my rose

More than a Pretty Face

The beauty inside her shines brighter
than her pretty face ever could.
How she looks on the inside will take her
further than the outside ever would.
Her compassion, genuine love, and positive attitude
are what make her glow.
Her caring spirit and her gleaming personality
will always steal the show.
Her outer reflection doesn't determine
all the things she is meant to be.
It is her determination
that will lead her to her destiny.
So when she looks in the mirror,
she gazes upon the beautiful traits she embodies
that run deeper than the surface of her skin.
She realizes her pretty face is yet a bonus
to her flawless beauty within.

Younger me

FLOURISHING FORWARD

"Your faith is your title deed. It says you have what God says you have."

JOURNAL ENTRY

"...My Uncle Wayne keeps telling me to write, so here I am, writing. My Ma Ma used her journal to write her very first book, 'Learning Within these Walls', so maybe I'll use the same concept. I'm just ready for it. Whatever happens, as long as it's in God's will for my life, I'm happy with it!"

Love Yours

Love starts at home.
Love comes from within.
Love yourself first,
Then you may love again.

TY, N

(spoken over Ariana Grande's 'thank u, next")

Thought I'd end up with Ron,

but we weren't the best match.

Wrote some poems about Vibey,

now I listen and laugh.

Marcus made me a mommy,

and for her, I'm so thankful.

Now I'm giving my love to Charlee;

she is my angel.

One taught me love,

one taught me patience,

one taught me pain,

now I'm so amazing.

I've loved, and I've lost,

but that's not all that I see…

I've loved, and I've lost.

Never knew how much it'd cost.

But I know that I've lost a lot,

and at times it felt

like all I had left to give

was a broken heart.

I've loved, and I've lost,

never knew how much it'd cost me.

But in my reflection, I see her

and I see that I've been reimbursed

by falling in love with myself

and that is what it's bought me.

"Poetry comes from the highest happiness or the deepest sorrow."
-APJ Abdul Kalam

I Know Who She Is

I know who she is.
I know who she has been.

I know I have the power
to let her be all that she can be.
And all that only she can be.

Eye know because I am her
and she is me.

"The accountability I lacked was holding me back."
-Starlito

Know Yourself

No one knows me as well as I know myself.
And to be honest, that used to frighten me.
It took courage to fall in love with myself.
Because falling in love with myself
meant falling in love with my whole self.
Flaws and ALL.
The good, the bad, the hurt, the past, and the ugly.
It takes courage
to face the pain.
It takes courage
to face the hard truths.
It takes courage to break bad habits and cycles.
It takes courage to not give up on myself.
It takes courage
to get back up again,
knowing that I have failed myself
time after time.
It takes courage.
The courage I have had within
since the start of my journey.
Circumstances didn't build the courage.
It was in me all along.
I just have to act in it.
I am proud of myself for finally applying the courage.

Growing Pains

Growing pains.

Alone again.

Why am I so afraid?

Good-Good

I got real good lovin'
Loving that's so good,
sometimes, I'm too good a woman.

I'm a good mother,
a good friend,
I give good advice.
I'm a good partner to have, and I pray I make a good wife.
Good credit,
good work ethic,
I can cook a good meal.
Got the ambition
to run up a million, too.
I pay all my bills.
I got real good lovin' Loving that's so good,
I know that I am too good a woman.

I Am Loved

I am loved,
I am cared for,
I am healed,
and I am whole.

Heartbreak will not get the best of me.
I gave my all to love,
And now I'm stuck here
with the rest of me.
I need it all back.

JOURNAL ENTRY

"Looking back at some of these decade-old journal entries, I see how far I've come. So much has changed, and all good things. One of the best things is that I am now a mother. I birthed a beautiful baby girl on December 6, 2022, at 6:38 AM, weighing 7.10 lbs, and she brings me unspeakable joy. She has taught me so much in her few years of life. When I decided to have my baby, knowing that I would be a single mother, I vowed to make better decisions from that point forward. I have grown from a girl to a woman, noting that the true essence of womanhood lies in the way you carry yourself. In 2014, I noticed I wasn't living right and attempted to navigate back to holiness, but ultimately ended up spending the next 10 years of my life distracted. The girl I was before had lost herself and been broken. It wasn't until I turned 30 last year that I began to mature into who I am today, giving all glory to God. My auntie Debra always said, "It's something about 30," and boy, was she right. I felt a shift happening in my life. I slowly began to see myself the way God sees me, not letting my past mistakes determine my future, nor who I am. I have begun to release. Dead weight, situations, and people who no longer serve me. The desire to be chosen, because God has already chosen me, so it doesn't matter who does or doesn't. The habit of trying to control the things I can't which has been a game-changer for me. So now, at 31, I am headed where I am supposed to be. Anticipating the blessings of each day, I speak life and positivity over myself. I am making healthier choices consistently and intentionally. I am a child and friend of God. I pray I will be a wife. I am a mother, a daughter, a sister, a poet, an author, a student, and a friend, and I aspire to be an educator one day. My advice, in its simplest form, is to keep learning, keep growing, and most importantly, keep on, never stop, and always remember to LOVE YOURSELF."

Rooted

I am rooted.

Just as a tree.

I am rooted in love, I am rooted in my beliefs.

And that is how come,

or should I say,

That is why

I have the wisdom not to stray.

At least not too far away.

From the roots.

The roots in which were grounded for me.

Long before me.

AUTHOR'S NOTE

For a while, I sat on my gift as a poet. I had multiple people speak to me about collecting my writing, but it wasn't until I desired it for myself that I began to walk into my purpose, using faith as my crutch. Many times, I had become discouraged and doubted my calling, thinking that I had waited too long and that God had used another vessel. I spent a lot of time being distracted. Distracted by social media, failed relationships, and allowing comparison to steal my joy.

During the COVID-19 pandemic, entrepreneurship skyrocketed, and I witnessed many of my peers begin to offer a range of goods and services for sale. I brainstormed and thought about what I could sell. Which products can I purchase in bulk and then flip to make a profit? One day, it came to me. You already have the product. The product is my talent in writing. I was looking outward, thinking I needed to buy a product, when I realized I already had the inventory within me and that the gift was free.

A short period of time later, my pastor spoke about a 'second wind.' He said that in this season, God has blessed us with a second wind and that it's time to set sail. I took heed to that, and I began to invest in myself as a poet. I began to tithe and pray for my purpose, and before I knew it, opportunities were coming my way.

That is what has led me here today. I encourage you to seek your purpose in life, discover the gifts God has given each of us, and use them to build your success.

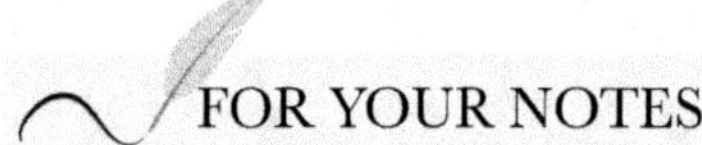

FOR YOUR NOTES

ABOUT THE AUTHOR

Cherish Cleveland has been writing for as long as she can remember. Long before she knew what poetry was, she understood what it felt like. Words became a refuge early on—a way to name the world when it felt too heavy to hold. Storytelling runs deep in her bloodline; with both a grandmother and an aunt as authors, language has always been an inheritance shaped by memory, survival, and care.

Raised by her maternal grandparents in a working-class, close-knit community, Cherish grew up surrounded by love, resilience, and a deep reverence for people. While material resources were limited, imagination was abundant. There was never a rigid career plan—only a quiet certainty that she wanted to change the world, and that words would be her way in.

Now studying Creative Writing, Cherish writes at the intersection of memory, faith, and becoming. Her work is deeply personal and spiritually reflective, shaped by lived experience and inspired by writers such as Toni Morrison, whose reverence for Black interior life continues to guide her voice. She aspires to be a poet, educator, and songwriter—someone who teaches, sings, and writes truth into rooms that need it.